T0086993

Breath of Song

10 works by women composers for unaccompanied SATB choir

Compiled and edited by
SARAH QUARTEL

MUSIC DEPARTMENT
OXFORD
UNIVERSITY PRESS

OXFORD
UNIVERSITY PRESS

Great Clarendon Street, Oxford OX2 6DP,
United Kingdom

Oxford University Press is a department of the University of Oxford.
It furthers the University's objective of excellence in research, scholarship,
and education by publishing worldwide. Oxford is a registered trade mark of
Oxford University Press in the UK and in certain other countries

© Oxford University Press 2021

Sarah Quartel has asserted her right under the Copyright, Designs
and Patents Act, 1988, to be identified as the Compiler and Editor of this anthology

Each composer has asserted her right under the Copyright, Designs
and Patents Act, 1988, to be identified as the Composer of their Work

Database right Oxford University Press (maker)

First published 2021

Impression: 1

All rights reserved. No part of this publication may be reproduced,
stored in a retrieval system, or transmitted, in any form or by any means,
without the prior permission in writing of Oxford University Press

Permission to perform this work in public (except in the course of divine worship)
should normally be obtained from a local performing right licensing organization,
unless the owner or the occupier of the premises being used already holds
a licence from such an organization. Likewise, permission to make and
exploit a recording must be obtained in advance from a
local mechanical copyright licensing organization

Enquiries concerning reproduction outside the scope of the above
should be directed to the Music Rights Department, Oxford University Press, at
music.permissions.uk@oup.com or at the address above

ISBN 978-0-19-353202-1

Music and text origination by Julia Bovee
Printed in Great Britain on acid-free paper by
Halstan & Co. Ltd, Amersham, Bucks.

Preface

In response to a growing demand for pieces by women composers, I was invited by Oxford University Press to assemble a collection of outstanding new works from living contributors. This set me on an exciting journey of discovery as I sought out new composers from across the world and had the opportunity to connect with others I've long admired.

Breath of Song brings together ten compelling works from different creators, some of whom are well-known, and others are just beginning to make their mark on the international choral scene. Each piece contributed to shaping this collection and played a part in refining the parameters of the original brief. In *Breath of Song* we have a group of unaccompanied works appropriate for concert performance and at a difficulty level accessible to the majority of choirs. Sacred and secular texts are both represented, and pieces can be programmed individually or together in one thrilling concert. Each work has a unique story to tell and brings something fresh and exciting to the contemporary choral catalogue. From the modal sound coloured by the Hindustani classical tradition in Esmail's 'TāReKiṬa', to the expressive melodic lines seasoned with Scottish snaps in McDowall's 'God be with us', there is something in this eclectic collection for each choir, each concert, and each season.

Thank you to Robyn Elton, Commissioning Editor at Oxford University Press, for her tireless work on this project and for amplifying voices that deserve to be heard. Thank you to Amy Chang and Jane Griffiths for keen eyes and thoughtful editing. Finally, thank you to my fellow composers for sharing your music and for trusting us with your exquisite work.

Sarah Quartel
November 2020

Contents

Notes on the pieces vi

Wake, Love, Wake! *Joan Szymko* 1

My beloved spake *Becky McGlade* 6

God be with us *Cecilia McDowall* 16

TāReKiṬa *Reena Esmail* 22

Love Letter *Sarah Dacey* 33

The Arrow and the Song *Laura Hawley* 40

The Birds' Lullaby *Sarah Quartel* 56

Snow is Silent *Jenny Mahler* 64

O ye who taste that Love is sweet *Eleanor Daley* 75

Round me falls the night *Annabel Rooney* 80

Notes on the pieces

Wake, Love, Wake! *Joan Szymko*

This is an emotive and rich setting of an exquisite text by Rabindranath Tagore. There is tremendous opportunity for word-painting right from the beginning. Feeling and expressing the emotion behind each word will make for an impactful singing experience and moving performance. Though much of the piece is marked ***pp***, ***p***, and ***mp***, there is room for great range within these dynamics. Use consonants to project and help keep the sound lifted in quieter moments. Relaxing into the end of descending phrases will allow the music to land with the text and the piece's impactful message to be felt.

My beloved spake *Becky McGlade*

McGlade's setting of this well-known passage from Song of Songs is warm and evocative. Moments of tenderness and intimacy in the text are brought to the fore as singers maintain connectivity by breathing together at the same speed, and moving as one through moments of subtle tempo change. Take care with triplets throughout, ensuring that enough time is given and they are not rushed. Excellent in a concert setting, this piece is suitable for a larger group as well as an unconducted small ensemble.

God be with us *Cecilia McDowall*

'God be with us' has a graceful and meditative quality. Expressive and flowing melodic lines float between voices creating a gentle sense of push and pull. Use the breath throughout to keep the sound buoyant and to support the stillness and sustain found in the writing. Notice the contrast between the legato lines and the clear rhythm of the Scotch snaps. Always accent the snaps, as is noted in the score. There are many moments to enjoy—relax into dissonances and lean into suspensions. This piece would be suitable in both liturgical and concert settings.

TāReKiṬa *Reena Esmail*

This is an exciting piece that feels tremendously satisfying to sing when performance is rooted in knowing it deeply. It is in a rāga (a melodic framework similar to a mode) called Jog, which incorporates both major and minor modalities into a single scale. The text syllables are onomatopoeic vocalizations of the sounds produced by Hindustani (north Indian classical) instruments. At first glance the text may look daunting to those unfamiliar with these vocalizations but, at closer look, you will see that there are only three different patterns of text throughout the piece. These patterns are easy to master when learned by ear and repeated aloud. Instructions detailing how to access the composer's video pronunciation guide can be found in the score. This piece would make a bright and energizing close to any concert.

Love Letter *Sarah Dacey*

'Love Letter' is set in a gently rocking 5/8 metre and features captivating harmonic language that is intriguing yet accessible. The light divisi in soprano and alto parts is well within the reach of community choirs. Watch that the opening 'mm' is not a percussive 'hmm' but rather embodies a warm and supportive foundation. Close attention to dynamics throughout, particularly on the first page, will help capture the ebb and flow in the writing by placing weight and understanding on significant words in the text.

The Arrow and the Song *Laura Hawley*

With a strong melody and a grooving rhythmic accompaniment, 'The Arrow and the Song' is a distinctive setting of Longfellow's text that is very satisfying to sing. Equally enjoyable in the hands of a small ensemble or full choir, this piece is set in a contemporary *a cappella* style with some pop inflections. In passages with ostinati, be careful to maintain pitch integrity by keeping lift and spin in the voice. It may be helpful for singers to notice how their riff is reframed when the harmony underneath changes while their ostinato remains the same.

The Birds' Lullaby *Sarah Quartel*

This is a playful yet tender piece with a singable melody and dancing scat accompaniment. It would work well for either full choir or a small ensemble. In the chorus section, go right to the 'ng' sound on 'sing' and 'swing' to keep the music rhythmic and light. Take care to remain casual on the 'd' of 'doo' and do not enunciate crisply. It should feel free and easy. This piece would work well on any programme celebrating nature, spring, or Earth Day.

Snow is Silent *Jenny Mahler*

This dynamic and engaging piece is filled with character. The excitement of the work is deepened through the use of body percussion, quick contrasting dynamics, and passages with vocal sound effects. Experiment with the placement of singers in the performance space to further enjoy the dramatic possibilities of the piece. Pay attention to how the composer has set vibrant words in the text such as 'kerfuffle', 'commotion', and 'splash'. Be sure to follow all articulations, dynamics, and written instructions in order to capture the full effect. This work would be excellent as a conclusion to a first half or as a concert closer.

O ye who taste that Love is sweet *Eleanor Daley*

This hymn-like setting of Christina Rossetti's secular text about love would be meaningful at a wedding or within a concert programmed around a variety of themes, including Christmas. While not difficult, the work is expertly crafted with each voice receiving an engaging part. Creative staging such as singing in the round or from a balcony would be comfortable and attainable with this piece. Maintain the air-flow through rising sections of eighth notes and move here with breath-filled propulsion, rather than acceleration.

Round me falls the night *Annabel Rooney*

The atmosphere is instantly set in the opening bars of this shining piece. One can immediately envision a beautiful evening emerging as the brightness of day softens into dusk. Rooney makes excellent use of the full range of all voice types, capitalizing on colours available in higher versus lower registers. Be sure to keep the vowel light in words such as 'done' and 'none' which sit lower in the range. Enjoy the harmonic shifts throughout and bring out moments in which one voice moves in a contrasting rhythm from the others. This piece would be lovely in both church and concert settings.

Sarah Quartel

All of the pieces in this anthology are also available separately from the OUP website and participating digital retailers.

Wake, Love, Wake!

Rabindranath Tagore
(1861–1941)

JOAN SZYMKO
(b. 1957)

Duration: 3 mins

© Oxford University Press 2020. Photocopying this copyright material is ILLEGAL.

a tempo
pp
p
Wake, O Pain of Love, Wake, O Pain of Love,
Wake, O Pain of Love, Wake, O Pain of Love,
Wake, O Pain of Love, Wake, O Pain of Love,
Wake, O Pain of Love, Wake, O Pain of Love,
a tempo
pp
poco più mosso ♩ = 62
rit.
mf
mp
Wake, O Pain of Love, for I know not how to o-pen the door.
Wake, O Pain of Love, and I stand out-side.
Wake, O Pain of Love, for I know not how to o-pen the door.
Wake, O Pain of Love, the door.
poco più mosso ♩ = 62
rit.

15
Tempo I (♩ = 54)
poco rit.
The hours wait, the stars watch, the wind is
The hours wait, the stars watch, the wind is
The hours wait, the stars watch, the wind is
The hours wait, watch, the wind is
Tempo I (♩ = 54)
poco rit.
19
poco meno mosso ♩ = 48 (♪ = ♪)
molto sostenuto
still, the si - lence is hea - vy, the si - lence is hea - vy,
still, the si - lence is hea - vy, the si - lence is hea - vy,
still, the si - lence is hea - vy, the si - lence is hea - vy,
still, the si - lence is hea - vy, the si - lence is hea - vy,
poco meno mosso ♩ = 48 (♪ = ♪)

23
molto rit.
the si - lence is hea - vy in my heart.
the si - lence is hea - vy in my heart.
the si - lence is hea - vy in my heart.
the si - lence is hea - vy in my heart.
molto rit.
26
Buoyant ♪ = 80
Tempo I (𝅗𝅥 = 54)
pp
p
mf
Wake, Love, Love, wake! brim my emp - ty cup,
Wake, Love, Love, wake! brim my emp - ty cup,
Wake, Love, Love, wake! brim my emp - ty cup,
Wake, Love, Love, wake! brim my emp - ty cup,
Buoyant ♪ = 80
Tempo I (𝅗𝅥 = 54)
pp
p
mp
mf

30
mp
mf
brim my emp - ty cup, fill my emp - ty cup,
brim my emp - ty cup, fill my emp - ty cup, and
brim my emp - ty cup, fill my cup,
brim my emp - ty cup, fill my cup,
34
p
and with a breath of song ruf - fle the night.
with a breath of song ruf - fle the night.
a breath of song ruf-fle the night.
of song ruf - fle the night.

My beloved spake

Song of Songs 2: 10–12

BECKY McGLADE
(b. 1974)

Duration: 3.5 mins

© Oxford University Press 2020. Photocopying this copyright material is ILLEGAL.

9
up, my love, rise up, my fair one,
up, my love, rise up, my fair one,
up, my love, rise up, my fair one,
up, my love, rise up, my fair one,
13
f
mp
rise up, my fair one, and come a -
rise up, my fair one, and come a -
rise up, my fair one, and come a -
rise up, my fair one, and come a -

17
-way, come a - way,
-way, come a - way,
-way, come a - way, a -
-way, come a - way,
20
a - way, a - way.
a - way, a - way.
mf
-way, a - way, a - way, a - way. For,
a - way, a - way.
mp

24
mp
mf
ah
ah
For,
mp
mf
ah
ah
For,
lo, the win - ter is past, the rain is o - ver and gone, For,
mp
mf
ah
ah
For,
mf
28
lo, the win - ter is past, the rain is o - ver and
lo, the win - ter is past, the rain is o - ver and
lo, the win - ter is past, the rain is o - ver and
lo, the win - ter is past, the rain is o - ver and

32
p
mp cresc.
gone, o - ver and gone; The flow'rs ap -
p
mp
cresc.
gone, o - ver and gone; The flow'rs ap - pear on the
p
mp cresc.
gone, o - ver and gone; The flow'rs ap -
mp
cresc.
gone; The flow'rs ap - pear on the
p
mp
cresc.
36
f
- pear on the earth; and the time of the
f
earth, on the earth; and the time of the
f
- pear on the earth; and the time of the
f
earth, on the earth; and the time of the
f

39
S.1
sing - ing of birds is come,
S.2
sing - - ing of birds is come,
A.
sing - - ing of birds is come,
T.
mp
sing - - ing of birds is come, and the voice of the
B.
sing - - ing of birds is come.
mp
43
p
heard, heard in our land.
p
heard, heard in our land,
p
heard, heard in our land,
tur - tle is heard, heard in our land,
mp
A -
p

47
mf
A - rise,
in our land, our land. A - rise,
mp
in our land, our land. A - rise,
in our land, our land. A -
-rise, a - rise, a -
51
f
a - rise.
rall.
a tempo
p
Rise
-rise, a - rise.
-rise, a - rise.

54
S.
up, my love, rise up, my
A.
up, my love, rise up, my
T.
up, my love, rise up, my
B.
up, my love, rise up, my
57
f
fair one, rise up, my fair
fair one, rise up, my fair
fair one, rise up, my fair
fair one, rise up, my fair

60
mp
one, and come a - way,
one, and come a - way,
one, and come a - way,
one, and come a - way,
mp
63
p
come a - way, a - way,
come a - way, a - way,
come a - way, come a - way, a - way, come a-
come a - way, a - way,

67
S.1
mf
mp
come a - way, a -
S.2
mf
mp
a - way, come a - way,
A.
mf
mp
a - way, a - way, a - way, come a -
T.
mf
mp
-way, a - way, a - way,
B.
mf
mp
a - way, a - way,
71
meno mosso
-way, come a - way, come a - way.
come a - way, come a - way.
-way, come a - way, come a - way.
come a - way, come a - way.
come a - way, come a - way.
meno mosso

for Val Withams

God be with us

Invocation, *Carmina Gadelica*, Vol. 1
Alexander Carmichael
(1832–1912)

CECILIA McDOWALL
(b. 1951)

* Sing as Scotch snaps, always clearly accented.

Duration: 2.5 mins

© Oxford University Press 2021. Photocopying this copyright material is ILLEGAL.

5
mf
mp
with us On this Thy night, To us and with us
with us On this Thy night, To us and
with us On this Thy night, this Thy night,
with us On this Thy night,
10
On this Thy day, A - men, To us and
with us On this Thy day, A - men, To
To us and with us On
To us and with us,

15
mp
p
mf
with us On this Thy night, A - men. It is
us and with us On this night, A - men. God be
this Thy night.
mp
p mf
A - - men. God be
mf
20
clear to be seen of us, Since we came
with us On this Thy day, God be with us
mf
It is clear to be seen of us, Since
with us On this Thy day, God be with us

24
f
mf
in - to the world, That we have de - served Thy
On this Thy night, To us and with us
we came in - to the world, in - to the world, That we have de -
On this Thy night, To us
29
wrath, A - men. O Thine own wrath, Thou
On this Thy day, A - men. To us and with us
- served Thy wrath, A - men. O Thine own
and with us, A -

34
p dolce
God of all, A - men. ah
p dolce
On this night, A - men. ah
p dolce
wrath, Thou God of all, A - men. ah
p
mf espress.
- - men. Grant us for - give-ness, A -
p dolce
39
mf
mp
ah ah
mf
mp
ah ah
mf
mp mf
ah A - - men. Thou
f
mp
- men. Grant to us Thine own for - give - ness,
mf
mf

45
mp
mf cresc.
ah
ah
mp
mf cresc.
To us and with us On this Thy day, A - men. Grant
mer - ci - ful God of all, A - men, A - men. ah
mp
mf cresc.
Grant us for - give - ness ev - er -
mp
mf cresc.
50
f
rit. poco a poco
p
ah A - men.
f
p
us for - give - ness ev - er - more, A - men.
f
p
To us and with us On this night, A - men.
f
p
- more, A - - - - men.
rit. poco a poco
f
p

For a video pronunciation guide led by Reena Esmail, please visit www.oup.co.uk/tarekita

PRONUNCIATION GUIDE

Vowels
ā as in c**a**r
a as in **a**bout
e as in f**e**d
i as in s**i**t
ī as in tr**ee**
ō as in n**o**te
ŭ as in g**oo**d
u as in th**u**mb
ū as in f**oo**d

Consonants (when different from English pronunciation)
t as in **th**e (dental) *
d as in the Spanish word **d**os or **d**ón**d**e (dental)
r as in the Spanish word **r**ojo or **r**osa (flipped)

Sounds with no equivalents in Romance languages
To make the sound "Dh":
- touch your tongue to your teeth, as if you were saying the word "the" (dental consonant)
- as you say the consonant, push extra air through it (if you hold your palm a few inches in front of your mouth, you should be able to feel a puff of air)

To make the sound "ṭ":
- curl your tongue back, so the underside of the tip is touching the top of your mouth (retroflex consonant)
- then bring it forward to pronounce the ṭ

* The "t" is the most critical consonant to pronounce correctly in this piece. If one singer in the choir uses a conventional English "t" sound, it will drown out the subdued attack of all the other dental "t"s.

for Urban Voices Project

TāReKiṬa
(तारेकिट)

Words and music by
REENA ESMAIL
(b. 1983)

* close to m immediately

Duration: 2 mins

© Oxford University Press 2021. Photocopying this copyright material is ILLEGAL.

* Grace notes should only be sung by a few singers per section.

21
nā nā nā nā
Dhā tā - re - ki - ṭa Dhŭm tā - re - ki - ṭa Nōm tā - re - ki - ṭa Ta - ka - dī - mī - ta - ka
Dhā tā - re - ki - ṭa Dhŭm tā - re - ki - ṭa Nōm tā - re - ki - ṭa Ta - ka - dī - mī - ta - ka
Hum tā nā nā
25
nā nā nā nā
Dhā tā - re - ki - ṭa Dhŭm tā - re - ki - ṭa Nōm tā - re - ki - ṭa Ta - ka - dī - mī - ta - ka
Dhā tā - re - ki - ṭa Dhŭm tā - re - ki - ṭa Nōm tā - re - ki - ṭa Ta - ka - dī - mī - ta - ka
Hum tā nā nā
29
mf
nā ja - nū Ta - ka - dī - mī
Dhā tā - re - ki - ṭa Dhŭm tā - re - ki - ṭa Nōm tā - re - ki - ṭa Ta - ka - dī - mī - ta - ka
mf
Dhā tā - re - ki - ṭa Dhŭm tā - re - ki - ṭa Ta - ka - dī - mī Ta - ka - ja - nū Ta - ka - dī - mī
Hum tā nā nā

33
f
Nā nā nā nā nā
f mp
Dhā tā - re - ki - ṭa Dhŭm tā - re - ki - ṭa Nōm tā - re - ki - ṭa Ta - ka - dī - mī - ta - ka
f mp
Dhā tā - re - ki - ṭa Dhŭm tā - re - ki - ṭa Nōm tā - re - ki - ṭa Ta - ka - dī - mī - ta - ka
f mp
Hum tā nā nā
37
nā nā nā nā
Dhā tā - re - ki - ṭa Dhŭm tā - re - ki - ṭa Nōm tā - re - ki - ṭa Ta - ka - dī - mī - ta - ka
Dhā tā - re - ki - ṭa Dhŭm tā - re - ki - ṭa Nōm tā - re - ki - ṭa Ta - ka - dī - mī - ta - ka
Hum tā nā nā
41
nā nā nā nā nā
Dhā tā - re - ki - ṭa Dhŭm tā - re - ki - ṭa Nōm tā - re - ki - ṭa Ta - ka - dī - mī - ta - ka
Dhā tā - re - ki - ṭa Dhŭm tā - re - ki - ṭa Nōm tā - re - ki - ṭa Ta - ka - dī - mī - ta - ka
Hum tā nā nā

* Low basses may sing an octave lower for the remainder of the piece, if desired.

57
Dhā tā - re - ki - ṭa Dhŭm tā - re - ki - ṭa Nōm tā - re - ki - ṭa Ta - ka - dī - mī - ta - ka
Hum
Ta - ka - dī - mī - ta - ka
Hum
Hum
tā nā nā
61
Dhā tā - re - ki - ṭa Dhŭm tā - re - ki - ṭa Tā ja - nū Ta - ka - dī - mī
mf
Hum
Ta - ka - dī - mī Ta - ka - ja - nū Ta - ka - dī - mī
mf
Hum
Ta - ka - dī - mī Ta - ka - ja - nū Ta - ka - dī - mī
Hum
tā nā nā
65
f
Nā nā nā
f mp
Dhā tā - re - ki - ṭa Dhŭm tā - re - ki - ṭa Nōm tā - re - ki - ṭa Ta - ka - dī - mī - ta - ka
f
Tā Nā
Hum
tā nā nā

69
nā nā nā nā
Dhā tā - re - ki - ṭa Dhŭm tā - re - ki - ṭa Nōm tā - re - ki - ṭa Ta - ka - dī - mī - ta - ka
nā nā nā
Hum tā nā nā
73
nā nā nā nā
Dhā tā - re - ki - ṭa Dhŭm tā - re - ki - ṭa Nōm tā - re - ki - ṭa Ta - ka - dī - mī - ta - ka
nā nā nā nā
Hum tā nā nā
77
mf
nā ja - nū Ta - ka - dī - mī
Dhā tā - re - ki - ṭa Dhŭm tā - re - ki - ṭa Nōm tā - re - ki - ṭa Ta - ka - dī - mī - ta - ka
mf
nā nā nā Ta - ka - dī - mī Ta - ka - ja - nū Ta - ka - dī - mī
Hum tā nā nā

81
f
Nā nā nā nā nā
f
Dhā tā - re - ki - ṭa Dhŭm tā - re - ki - ṭa Nōm tā - re - ki - ṭa Ta - ka - dī - mī - ta - ka
f
Nā nā
Hum tā nā nā
85
nā nā nā nā
Dhā tā - re - ki - ṭa Dhŭm tā - re - ki - ṭa Nōm tā - re - ki - ṭa Ta - ka - dī - mī - ta - ka
nā nā nā nā nā
Hum tā nā nā
89
nā nā nā nā nā
Dhā tā - re - ki - ṭa Dhŭm tā - re - ki - ṭa Nōm tā - re - ki - ṭa Ta - ka - dī - mī - ta - ka
nā nā nā nā nā
Hum tā nā nā

93
Dhā tā - re - ki - ṭa Dhŭm tā - re - ki - ṭa Nōm tā - re - ki - ṭa Ta - ka - dī - mī - ta - ka
Dhā
nā nā nā na
Hum
tā nā nā
97
p
Dhā tā - re - ki - ṭa Dhŭm tā - re - ki - ṭa Nōm tā - re - ki - ṭa Ta - ka - dī - mī - ta - ka
Dīm tā - nā - nā Nōm tā - nā - nā Nŭm tā - nā - nā tā nā nā
Dīm tā - nā - nā Nōm tā - nā - nā Nŭm tā - nā - nā tā nā nā
Hum
tā nā nā
101
mp
Dhā tā - re - ki - ṭa Dhŭm tā - re - ki - ṭa Nōm tā - re - ki - ṭa Ta - ka - dī - mī - ta - ka
Dīm tā - nā - nā Nōm tā - nā - nā Nŭm tā - nā - nā tā nā nā
Dīm tā - nā - nā Nōm tā - nā - nā Nŭm tā - nā - nā tā nā nā
Hum
tā nā nā

105
mf
f
Dhā tā - re - ki - ṭa Dhŭm tā - re - ki - ṭa Nōm tā - re - ki - ṭa Ta - ka - dī - mī - ta - ka Dhā tā - re - ki - ṭa
Dīm tā - nā - nā Nōm tā - nā - nā Nŭm tā - nā - nā tā nā nā Dhā tā - re - ki - ṭa
Dīm tā - nā - nā Nōm tā - nā - nā Nŭm tā - nā - nā tā nā nā Hum
Hum tā nā nā Hum
110
Ta - ka - dī - mī - ta - ka Dhā tā - re - ki - ṭa Ta - ka - dī - mī - ta - ka Dhā tā - re - ki - ṭa
Ta - ka - dī - mī - ta - ka Dhā tā - re - ki - ṭa Ta - ka - dī - mī - ta - ka Dhā tā - re - ki - ṭa
tā nā nā Hum tā nā nā Hum
tā nā nā Hum tā nā nā Hum
114
Ta - ka - dī - mī - ta - ka Ta - ka - dī - mī Ta - ka - ja - nū Ta - ka - dī - mī Dhā Dhā Dhā
Ta - ka - dī - mī - ta - ka Hum Dhā Dhā Dhā
tā nā nā Ta - ka - dī - mī Ta - ka - ja - nū Ta - ka - dī - mī Dhā Dhā Dhā
tā nā nā Hum Dhā Dhā Dhā

for Richard and Teresa

Love Letter

Edna St Vincent Millay
(1892–1950)

SARAH DACEY
(b. 1979)

Duration: 3 mins

© Oxford University Press 2021. Use of an excerpt from Edna St Vincent Millay's letter to Arthur Davison Ficke (24 January 1922) courtesy of the Millay Society (millay.org). Photocopying this copyright material is ILLEGAL.

* Keyboard reduction for rehearsal only.

Bouncy and insistent ♪ = 180
33
sub. mp
S.1
All that has no-thing to do, all that has no-thing to do with,
S.2
A.
f
love.
T.
f
love.
B.
f
love.
Bouncy and insistent ♪ = 180
f
sub. mp
37
all that has no-thing to do, all that has
mp
all that has no-thing to do, all that has no-thing to do with,

41
p legato
no-thing to do, all that has no-thing to do, all that has,
all that has no-thing to do, all that has no-thing to do with,
mp
ah ah ah ah
mp
ah ah ah ah
mp
ah ah ah ah
45
rall.
mf
all that has no-thing to do, all that has no-thing to do with
p legato
mf
all that has no-thing to do, all that has no-thing to do with
p
mf
ah ah ah ah
p
mf
ah ah ah ah
p
mf
ah ah ah ah
rall.
p
mf

49
Tempo II ♪ = 180
S.
what we are, what we are to each o - ther.
A.
What we are, what we are to each o - ther.
T.
What we are, what we are.
B.
What we are, what we are.
Tempo II ♪ = 180
55
S.
A.
Nor how of-ten, nor how of-ten, nor how of-ten,
T.
B.
mm mm mm mm mm mm mm
62
nor how of-ten, nor how sweet-ly, nor how sweet-ly, nor
mm mm mm mm mm mm

68
div.
ah
mf
S.
how sweet-ly, nor how sweet-ly. No - thing at all to do with
A.
how sweet-ly, nor how sweet-ly. ah No-thing at all to
T.
mm mm mm ah
B.
mm mm mm ah
73
unis.
you, no-thing at all to do with you, with
do with you and me, and no-thing at all to
No-thing at all to do with you, with you and
ah No-thing at all to do with

77
p
you and me, with you and me, you and me, you and
p
do with you and me, and me, you and me, you and
p
me, with you and me, and me, you and me, you and
p
you, with you and me, and me, you and me, you and
p

84
rit.
dim.
me, and me, you and me, you and you and
dim.
me, and me, and me, and you me, and me.
me, you and me.
me.
rit.
dim.

Commissioned in 2016 by the Savridi Singers of Calgary and their artistic director, Erica Phare-Bergh, for the occasion of the choir's 30th anniversary

The Arrow and the Song

Henry Wadsworth Longfellow
(1807–82)

LAURA HAWLEY
(b. 1982)

Before the notes begin, start with *c.*15–20 seconds of some voices imitating the sounds of wind, gentle breezes, the subtle whistle of an arrow, and occasional bird calls. Continue the wind and birds (or wind only) until the text begins in b. 13. Choirs should feel free to experiment with placement of singers, textural variety, and character and 'pitch' of the wind and bird sounds according to their own artistic expressive nuance.

* straight to the '*n*' of '*doon*'

† The piano reduction includes the rhythmic accompanying parts throughout; for reason of playability, melodic lines are sometimes omitted.

Also available separately in a version for SSSAAA unaccompanied (ISBN 978–0–19–355088–9).

Duration: 4 mins

© Oxford University Press 2021. Photocopying this copyright material is ILLEGAL.

* *'du'* should sound like *'doo'*

11
ALTO SOLO or SOLI mf
A. SOLO
I shot an ar - row in - to the
S.
doon doon du doon doon doon doon du doon doon doon doon du doon doon doon du doon
A.
doon doon doon doon doon
T.
dn dn dn dn dn dn dn dn dn dn dn dn
14
air, It fell to earth, I knew_ not where; For, so
doon doon du doon doon doon doon doon du doon doon doon doon_ du doon doon
doon doon doon doon doon
dn dn dn dn dn dn dn dn dn dn dn dn

17
swift - ly it flew, so swift - ly, the sight Could not fol - low,
doon doon du doon doon doon du doon doon doon du doon doon doon doon doon du doon doon
doon doon doon doon doon doon
dn dn dn dn dn dn dn dn dn dn dn dn
20
A. SOLO
fol-low in its flight.
S.
doon doon du doon doon doon doon du doon doon doon du doon doon doon
A.
doon doon doon doon doon
T.
dn dn dn doon doon du doon doon doon du doon doon doon du doon doon doon
BASS
mp
B.
dn dn dn dn dn dn dn dn dn

23
doon doon du doon doon doon doon du doon doon doon doon du doon doon doon du doon
doon doon doon doon doon
doon doon du doon doon doon doon du doon doon doo
dn dn dn dn dn dn dn dn dn dn dn dn

26
S.1
doon doon du doon doon doon doon doon du doon doon doon doon du doon doon
S.2
doon doon du doon doon doon doon doon du doon doon doon doon
A.
mf
doon doon doon doon
I
T.
3
doo doo doo doo doo
B.
dn dn dn dn dn dn dn dn dn dn dn dn
3

29
mp
doon doon du doon doon doon du doon doon doon du doon doon doon doon doon du doon doon
mp
doon doon doon doon doon
breathed a song in - to the air, It fell to earth, I knew not
mp lightly
I breathed a song in - to
mp
dn dn dn dn dn dn dn dn dn dn dn dn
32
poco a poco cresc.
doon doon du doon doon doon doon du doon doon doon du doon doon doon doon
poco a poco cresc.
doon doon doon doon doon
where; For who has sight so keen and strong, so
poco a poco cresc.
the air, who has sight so keen and
poco a poco cresc.
dn dn dn dn dn dn dn dn dn dn dn dn
poco a poco cresc.

35
ALTO SOLO or SOLI
mf
A. SOLO
So strong it can fol - low.
S.1
doon doon du doon doon doon doon du doon doon da da da da da da da da
S.2
doon doon doon doon da
A.
strong, That it can fol-low the flight of a song?
T.
strong, so strong it can fol - low.
B.
dn dn dn dn dn dn dn dn dn dn dn dn

38
da da da da da da da da da da da da da da da da da
da da da da da da da da da da da da da da da da da

42
S.1
da da da da da da da da da da da da
S.2
da da da da da da da da da da da da da da da da da
A.
da da
T.
da da da da da da da da da da da da da da da da
B.
doom doom doom doom doom doom doom doom doom doom doom doom
45
p
mp
oo
I found
mp
Long, long af - ter - ward,
I found the ar - row,
mp
Long, long af - ter-ward, in an oak
I found the ar - row, still un -
mp
I found the ar - row,
doom doom doom
p
ah
mp

49
poco a poco cresc.
the ar - row, and the song, I found a -
da
-broke; And the song, the song, from be - gin - ning to end, I
and the song, from be - gin - ning,
mp
doo doom doom da da da
52
f
-gain, a - gain in the heart,
da da in the heart, in the
found a - gain, a - gain in the heart, heart,
da da da da da the heart, ha
da I found a - gain in the heart,

56
ah
heart, in the heart,
heart da da da da da da da da da
da da da da da da da da da
heart, in the heart, the heart,
60
dim.
in the heart.
in the heart.
dim.
mf
doon doon doon doon doon doon doon doon doon doon of a friend.
in the heart.
in the heart of a friend.

64
mp
doon doon du doon doon doon du doon doon doon du doon doon doon
mm
doon doon du doon doon doon du doon doon doon du doon doon doon doon doon du doon doon
doon doon doon doon
dm dm dm dm dm dm dm dm dm dm dm dm
67
doon doon du doon doon doon doon du doon doon doon do doon doon doon du doon doon doon
doon doon doon doon doon
dm dm dm dm dm dm dm dm dm dm dm dm

70
A. SOLO
ALTO SOLO or SOLI mf
I shot an ar - row,
S.1
mm
mf
I
S.2
doon doon du doon doon doon doon du doon doon doon doon du doon doon doon du doon
A.
doon doon doon doon doo
T.
mf
dm dm dm dm dm dm dm
I shot an ar - row,
B.
dm dm dm dm dm

73
I shot an ar - row,
I
shot an ar - row,
I shot an ar - row,
doon doon du doon doon doon doon doon du doon doon doon doon du doon doon doo
doo doo doo doo
I
I shot an ar - row,
dm dm dm dm dm dm dm dm dm dm dm dm

76
shot an ar - row, I shot an ar - row,
I shot an ar - row, I
doo doo doo doo doo doo
shot an ar - row, I shot an ar - row,
I shot an ar - row, I shot an ar - row,
dm dm dm dm dm dm dm dm dm dm dm dm

* A few voices from each section leave the pitch and make the unvoiced wind sound: *'haaaaAAAaaaaah'*

The Birds' Lullaby

E. Pauline Johnson
(1861–1913)

SARAH QUARTEL
(b. 1982)

This piece is also available in a version for SSAA unaccompanied (ISBN 978–0–19–352466–8).

Duration: 3 mins

© Oxford University Press 2020. Photocopying this copyright material is ILLEGAL.

9
With sha-dow-y gar - ments, the wil-der-ness through;
doo doo doo doo doo doo doo doo doo doo doo doo doo doo doo doo
doo doo doo doo doo doo doo doo through;
doo doo doo doo doo doo doo doo doo doo doo doo doo doo doo doo
13
mf
All day we have ca - rolled, and now would be sleep-ing,
mp
doo doo doo doo doo doo doo doo doo doo doo doo doo doo doo doo
mp
doo doo doo doo doo doo doo doo doo doo doo doo doo doo doo doo
mp
doo doo doo doo doo doo doo doo doo doo doo doo doo doo doo doo
17
So e-cho the an - thems we war-bled to you; While we
doo doo doo doo doo doo doo doo you;
doo doo doo doo doo doo doo doo you;
doo doo doo doo doo doo doo doo you;

21
swing, And your branch - es sing, And we
Swing, swing, swing, swing, sing, sing, sing, sing,
Swing, swing, swing, swing, sing, sing, sing, sing,
Swing, swing, swing, swing, sing, sing, sing, sing,
25
mp
drowse to your dream - - - y whis - per - ing.
p
drowse, we drowse now, dream - y whisp'r - ing.
p
drowse, we drowse now, dream - y whisp'r - ing.
p
drowse, we drowse now, dream - y whisp'r - ing.
29
Sing to us now,
mp
doo doo doo doo doo doo doo doo Sing to us now,
mp
mf
Sing to us, ce - dars;
mp
Sing to us now,

33
night - wind sigh - ing, woo - ing, plead - ing,
night - wind sigh - ing, woo - ing, plead - ing,
the night - wind is sigh - ing, Is woo - ing, is plead - ing, to hear you re-
night - wind sigh - ing, woo - ing, plead - ing,
37
mf
you re - ply; da da da in your arms we are
mf
you re - ply; da da da in your arms we are
f
-ply; And here in your arms
mf
you re - ply; in your arms we are
41
ly - ing, da da da da da long - ing, dream - ing,
ly - ing, da da da da da long - ing, dream - ing,
we are rest - ful - ly ly - ing, And long-ing to dream to your soft
ly - ing, long - ing, dream - ing,

45
mp
lul - la - by; While we swing, And your branch-es
mp
lul - la - by; While we swing, swing, swing, swing,
mf
lul - la-by; While we swing, swing, swing, swing,
mp
lul - la - by; While we swing, swing, swing, swing,
49
mp
sing, And we drowse to your
sing, sing, sing, sing, drowse, we drowse now,
sing, sing, sing, sing, drowse, we drowse now,
sing, sing, sing, sing, drowse, we drowse now,
53
mp
dream - - - y whis - per ing. Sing to us, ce - dars;
p
p
dream - y whisp'r - ing. oh
p
p
dream - y whisp'r - ing. oh
p
p
dream - y whisp'r - ing. oh

57
your voice is so low - ly, Your breath-ing so fra-
oh
oh
oh
60
- grant, your branch-es so strong; Our lit - tle nest-
strong; oh
strong; oh
ah oh
64
- - cra - dles are sway - ing, so slow - ly,

67
While zeph-yrs are breath - ing their slumb'r - ous song.
oh
song.
oh
song.
oh
ah
poco rit.
slightly slower
70
mp
Swing, swing,
mp
Swing, swing,
mf
And we swing, While your branch-es
mp
swing, swing,
75
sing, sing, drowse,
sing, sing, drowse,
sing, And we drowse, and we
sing, sing, drowse,

79
f
drowse, And we swing, swing, While your
f
drowse, swing, swing,
f
drowse, swing, swing,
f
drowse, swing, swing,
83
mf
poco rit.
branch - es sing, And we drowse to your
mp
sing, sing, drowse,
mp
sing, sing, drowse,
mp
sing, sing, drowse,
87
mp
sempre rit.
dream - y whis-per-ing.
p
doo doo doo doo doo doo
p
oh doo doo doo doo doo doo doo doo doo doo doo
p
oh doo doo doo doo doo doo doo doo doo doo doo
p
oh doo doo doo doo doo doo doo doo doo doo doo

Snow is Silent

John Pickles
(b. 1953)

JENNY MAHLER
(b. 1989)

Duration: 2.5 mins

© Oxford University Press 2021. Photocopying this copyright material is ILLEGAL.

4
mf
f
O-ver val-leys, in the high-lands. Rain is noise.
O-ver val-leys, in the high-lands. Rain is noise.
O-ver val-leys, in the high-lands. Rain is noise.
O-ver val-leys, in the high-lands. Rain is noise.
9
sub. p
Rain is noise. Small ker-fuf-fle, great com-mo-tion,
Rain is noise. Small ker-fuf-fle, great com-mo-tion,
Rain is noise. Small ker-fuf-fle, great com-mo-tion,
Rain is noise. Small ker-fuf-fle, great com-mo-tion,
p

12
mf
Splash in pond, drop in o - cean. Rain is
Splash in pond, drop in o - cean. Rain is
Splash in pond, drop in o - cean. Rain is
Splash in pond, drop in o - cean. Rain is
mf
15
sfz
noise.
noise.
noise.
noise.
f
Rain is noise,
Rain is noise,

18
loud whisper
[palms]*
[click]**
Pit- ter, pat- ter, tip, tap, pit- ter, pat- ter,
sub. p
mf
Whe-ther fall-ing gent - ly,
[palms]*
loud whisper
pit- ter, pat- ter,
[palms]*
loud whisper
[click]**
f
Pit- ter, pat- ter, tip, tap, Or with
sub. p
mf
f
Whe-ther fall-ing gent - ly, Or with
p
mf
f
* = rub palms together
** = click fingers

† = stamp feet (left, right)

28
sh
Rain is noise.
sh
Rain is noise.
snow is si - lence.
A -
snow is si - lence.
A -
31
Feed - ing o - a - ses.
sub. p
Fall - ing, gen - tle, fall - ing, vio-
-wak'n-ing dor - mant seeds,
sub. p
Fall - ing, gen - tle, fall - ing, vio-
-wak'n-ing dor - mant seeds,

33
f cresc.
Rain is noise.
- lent. Rain is noise.
- lent. Rain is noise.
Rain is noise.
mp
But
f
36
mp
oh is si - lent.
f
Rain is noise.
oh is si - lent.
loud whisper
Snow is fast a - sleep!
oh snow is si - lent.
Snow is fast a - sleep!
softly spoken
Pit - ter, pat - ter,
snow, snow is si - lent.
Snow is fast a - sleep!

* straight to 'sh' of 'splash'

43
ff
Rain is the ma - gic po - tion the hea - vens weep.
ff
Rain is the ma - gic po - tion the hea - vens weep.
ff
Rain is the ma - gic po - tion the hea - vens weep.
ff
Rain is the ma - gic po - tion the hea - vens weep.
ff
46
mp cresc. poco a poco
Rain is noise, rain is noise, rain is noise, rain is noise,
mp cresc. poco a poco
Noise in mo-tion, noise in mo-tion, noise in mo-tion, noise
mp cresc. poco a poco

49
spoken p cresc. (continues throughout repeat)
Pit-ter, pat-ter, tip, tap, pit-ter, pat-ter, tip, tap,
rain is noise, rain is noise, rain is
spoken p cresc. (continues throughout repeat)
shouted
Pit-ter, pat-ter, tip, tap, pit-ter, pat-ter, tip, tap, pit-ter, pat-ter. Rain is noise!
in mo - tion, noise in mo - tion, noise in mo-tion,
51a
1.
2.
pit-ter, pat-ter, tip, tap, pit-ter, pat-ter, tip, tap. pit-ter, pat-ter, tip, tap, pit-ter, pat-ter, tip, tap,
noise, rain is noise, noise, rain is noise.
Pit-ter, pat-ter, rain is, Pit-ter, pat-ter, rain is,
noise in mo - tion, noise noise in mo - tion.
52
f
[stamp]
pitter, patter, tip, tap, pitter, patter, tip, tap, pitter, patter, tip, tap, pitter, patter, tip, tap.
spoken f
[stamp]
Tip, tap, pitter, patter, tip, tap, tip, tap, tip, tap, pitter, patter, tip, tap, tip, tap.
f
[stamp]
pitter, patter, tip, tap, pitter, patter, tap, pitter, patter, tip, tap, pitter, patter, tap.
spoken f
[stamp]
Tip, tap, tip, pitter, patter, tip, tap, tap, tip, tap, tip, pitter, patter, tip, tap, tap.

* ∿∿∿∿∿ = cacophony of clicks and thigh-slaps in free rhythm

Written for the wedding of Laura Pedersen and Christopher Bowman, 8 July 2006

O ye who taste that Love is sweet

Christina Rossetti
(1830–94)

ELEANOR DALEY
(b. 1955)

* Keyboard reduction for rehearsal only.

Duration: 3 mins

© Oxford University Press 2021. Photocopying this copyright material is ILLEGAL.

11
poco rit.
a tempo
mf
stum-ble on in search of it. Sing hymns of Love, sing hymns of Love, that
stum-ble on in search of it. Sing hymns of Love, sing hymns of Love, that
stum-ble on in search of it. Sing hymns of Love, sing hymns of Love, that
stum-ble on in search of it. Sing hymns of Love, sing hymns of Love, that
poco rit.
a tempo
mf
15
mp
those who hear far off in pain may lend an ear, rise
those who hear far off in pain may lend an ear, rise
those who hear far off in pain may lend an ear, rise
those who hear far off in pain may lend an ear, rise

19
rit.
a tempo
mf
up, rise up, rise up and won - der, and draw near. Lead lives of love, that
up, rise up, rise up and won - der, and draw near. Lead lives of love, that
up, rise up, and draw near. Lead lives of love, that
up, rise up, and draw near. Lead lives of love, that
25
o-thers who be - hold your lives may kin-dle too with Love, and cast their
o-thers who be - hold your lives may kin-dle too with Love, and cast their
o-thers who be - hold your lives may kin-dle too with Love, and cast their
o-thers who be - hold your lives may kin-dle too with Love, and cast their

29
poco rit.
a tempo
lots with you. Sing_ hymns of Love, sing_ hymns of Love, that_ those who hear_ far_
lots with you. Sing hymns of Love, sing hymns of Love, that those who hear_ far_
lots with you. Sing_ hymns of Love, sing hymns of Love, that those who hear far
lots with you. Sing_ hymns of Love, sing_ hymns of Love, that_ those who hear far
poco rit.
a tempo
33
mp
off in pain_ may_ lend_ an_ ear, rise up, rise up, rise
off in pain_ may_ lend_ an_ ear,_ rise up, rise up, rise
off in pain may_ lend_ an_ ear,_ rise up, rise up,
off in pain may lend an ear, rise up, rise up.

38
rit.
a tempo
p
up and won-der, and draw near.
oo
up and won-der, and draw near.
and draw near.
43
mp
O ye who taste that Love is sweet.
O ye who taste that Love is sweet.
O ye who taste that Love is sweet.
O ye who taste that Love is sweet.

Round me falls the night

William Romanis
(1824–99)

ANNABEL McLAUCHLAN ROONEY
(b. 1973)

Duration: 3 mins

Round me falls the night has been recorded by The Choir of Christ's College, Cambridge, conducted by David Rowland, on the album *As a seed bursts forth* (Regent).

© Oxford University Press 2021. Photocopying this copyright material is ILLEGAL.

6
mf
f
dark-ness shroud - ed Let me see thy face un - cloud - ed; Let thy glo - ry shine In this
dark-ness shroud - ed Let me see thy face un-cloud-ed; glo - ry shine,
dark - ness, Let me see thy face un - cloud - ed; Let thy glo - ry shine,
dark - ness, Let me see thy face; Let thy glo - ry shine,
10
p
mp
heart of mine. Earth - ly work is done, Earth - ly sounds are none;

15
p
pp
Rest in sleep and si-lence seek - ing, Let me hear thee soft-ly speak-ing; In my
Rest in sleep and si - lence, Let me hear thee soft-ly speak-ing; In my
Rest in sleep and si - lence, Let me hear thee soft - ly; In my
Rest in sleep and si - lence, Let me hear thee soft - ly; In my
19
mp
mf poco a poco cresc.
S.1
spi-rit's ear, 'I am near, I am near, I am near.'
S.2
mf sonore poco a poco cresc.
spi-rit's ear Whis-per, 'I am near.' Bless - èd, heav'n-ly Light,
A.
spi - rit's ear, 'I am near.' Bless - èd, heav'n-ly Light,
T.
spi - rit's ear, 'I am near.' Bless - èd, heav'n-ly Light,
B.
spi - rit's ear, 'I am near.' Bless - èd, heav'n-ly Light,

23
Shin - - - ing; Voice of love,
Shin - ing through earth's night; Voice, that oft of love
espress.
Shin - ing through earth's, shin - ing through earth's night; Voice, that oft of love
Shin - ing through earth's night; Voice, that oft, voice of
Shin - ing through earth's night; Voice, that oft of
26
voice of love, Arms, so strong to clasp and hold me; Thou thy watch wilt
hast told me; Arms, so strong to clasp and hold me; Thou thy watch wilt
hast told me; Arms, so strong to clasp and hold me; Thou thy watch wilt
love hast told me; Arms, so strong to clasp and hold me; Thou thy watch, thy
love hast told me; Arms, so strong to clasp and hold me; 'I am near, I am
espress.

30
p
mp espress.
keep, watch wilt keep, watch wilt keep, 'I am near, I am
keep, watch wilt keep, watch wilt keep, Sa - viour, o'er my sleep,
keep, watch wilt keep, watch wilt keep, Sa - viour, o'er my sleep,
watch wilt keep, Sa - viour, o'er my sleep,
mp
near, I am near.' Sa - viour, o'er my sleep,
34
rall.
SOPRANO SOLO
near.' 'I am near.'
pp
thou thy watch wilt keep, thy watch wilt keep.
thou thy watch wilt keep, thy watch wilt keep.
thou thy watch wilt keep, thy watch wilt keep.
thou thy watch wilt keep, thy watch wilt keep.
rall.